Lerner SPORTS

GREATEST OF ALL TIME PLAYERS

G.O.A.T. HOCKEY CENTERS

Josh Anderson

T0018693

Lerner Publications ◆ Minneapolis

SPORTS THRILLS *MEET* RESEARCH SKILLS

Lerner SPORTS

Free Database Trial: **lernersports.com**

Lerner Publications Company
An imprint of Lerner Publishing Group, Inc.
241 First Avenue North
Minneapolis, MN 55401 USA

For reading levels and more information, look up this title at www.lernerbooks.com.

Main body text set in Aptifer Sans LT Pro.
Typeface provided by Linotype AG.

Library of Congress Cataloging-in-Publication Data

Names: Anderson, Josh, author.
Title: G.O.A.T. hockey centers / Josh Anderson.
Other titles: Greatest of all time hockey centers
Description: Minneapolis, MN : Lerner Publications, [2024] | Series: Lerner sports. Greatest of all time players | Includes bibliographical references and index. | Audience: Ages 7–11 | Audience: Grades 2–3 | Summary: "Hockey centers are always in the middle of the action. Explore the careers of superstars such as Wayne Gretzky, Connor McDavid, and Hayley Wickenheiser. Who do you think is the greatest of all-time?"— Provided by publisher.
Identifiers: LCCN 2023017475 (print) | LCCN 2023017476 (ebook) | ISBN 9798765610237 (library binding) | ISBN 9798765623619 (paperback) | ISBN 9798765614907 (epub)
Subjects: LCSH: Hockey players—Canada—Biography—Juvenile literature. | Hockey players—United States—Biography—Juvenile literature. | Centers (Hockey)—Biography—Juvenile literature. | BISAC: JUVENILE NONFICTION / Biography & Autobiography / Sports & Recreation
Classification: LCC GV848.5.A1 A64 2024 (print) | LCC GV848.5.A1 (ebook) | DDC 796.962092/2—dc23/eng/20230420

LC record available at https://lccn.loc.gov/2023017475
LC ebook record available at https://lccn.loc.gov/2023017476

Manufactured in the United States of America
1 – CG – 12/15/23

TABLE OF CONTENTS

Sidney Crosby (lower right) of the Pittsburgh Penguins celebrates a big playoff goal against the Tampa Bay Lightning.

SAVING THE SEASON

The Pittsburgh Penguins won the Stanley Cup in 2009. They reached the National Hockey League (NHL) playoffs in each of the next six seasons. But they could not seem to win the Stanley Cup again. In the 2016 playoffs, the Penguins were losing three games to two. A loss to the Tampa Bay Lightning in Game 6 would end Pittsburgh's season.

The Penguins had a two-goal lead over the Lightning late in the second period. Pittsburgh right wing Patric Hörnqvist poked the

FACTS AT A GLANCE

» WAYNE GRETZKY'S 2,857 POINTS ARE THE MOST IN NHL HISTORY.

» EDMONTON OILERS CENTER CONNOR MCDAVID LED THE LEAGUE IN POINTS FIVE TIMES BETWEEN 2016 AND 2023.

» PHIL ESPOSITO OF THE BOSTON BRUINS HAD A RECORD 16 GAME-WINNING GOALS IN TWO DIFFERENT SEASONS.

» HALL OF FAMER JEAN BÉLIVEAU WON 10 STANLEY CUPS DURING HIS CAREER WITH THE MONTRÉAL CANADIENS.

puck away from a Lightning player. He passed it to center Sidney Crosby.

Crosby skated past two Lightning defenders on his way to the goal. Before a third defender could reach him, Crosby flicked the puck into the back of the net. Goal! The Penguins went on to win the game 5–2. One of the best centers to ever play hockey helped seal the victory. The Penguins later beat the San Jose Sharks to win the Stanley Cup.

Many hockey fans consider center to be the most important position. A center plays in the middle of the ice and covers more space than any other player. Centers control the pace of the game and lead their team's offense. They also try to stop the opposing team by playing tough defense.

Edmonton Oilers center Connor McDavid

Many fans consider center Wayne Gretzky to be the all-time best NHL player.

Centers often lead their teams in points. In the NHL, half of the top-10 career goal scorers have been centers. But which center was the greatest of all time (G.O.A.T.)? Let's find out.

CONNOR MCDAVID

The Edmonton Oilers picked Connor McDavid first overall in the 2015 NHL Draft. Many think he is the best skater and stickhandler in the NHL. He still has many years to play. But he's already one of the best to play the center position. McDavid led the NHL in points in five of his first eight seasons in the league. He is a strong leader on the ice and in the locker room. His teammates see how hard he works, and it inspires them to work harder as well. That's one reason McDavid became the youngest team captain in NHL history in 2016. He was only 19.

McDavid led the league in points three years in a row from 2021 through 2023. He is the first player to do this since Jaromír Jágr did it from 1998 to 2001. McDavid has also won the Hart Memorial Trophy twice. This award honors the NHL's Most Valuable Player (MVP).

CONNOR MCDAVID STATS

Points	850
Goals	303
Assists	547
NHL All-Star Games	6

Stats are accurate through the 2022–2023 NHL season.

HAYLEY WICKENHEISER

Many fans think of Hayley Wickenheiser as the greatest female hockey player of all time. She played for the Canada national team from 1993 to 2017. Between 1998 and 2014, Wickenheiser led Canada to four gold medals and one silver medal at the Winter Olympics. She won the tournament MVP award twice.

Wickenheiser also led Canada to seven gold medals and six silver medals at the Hockey World Championships. She is Team Canada's career points leader, with 168 goals and 211 assists. Wickenheiser also played softball for Canada at the 2000 Summer Olympics.

In 2003, the Hall of Famer became the first woman to play full-time on a men's pro hockey team in a position other than goalie. She was also the first woman to score a goal in a men's pro hockey league. In 2022, she became the assistant general manager of the Toronto Maple Leafs.

HAYLEY WICKENHEISER STATS

Points	379
Goals	168
Assists	211
Olympic Gold Medals	4

MARCEL DIONNE

Marcel Dionne played in the NHL for 18 seasons during the 1970s and 1980s. Playing center for the Los Angeles Kings, Dionne was part of the famous Triple Crown Line with wings Charlie Simmer and Dave Taylor. They earned the nickname for their amazing 1980–1981 season. All three players scored at least 100 points. No NHL team had ever had three players with 100 or more points in a season.

Dionne led the NHL with 137 points in 1979–1980. He ranks sixth all-time in points and goals. And his eight 100-point seasons are the third-most of all time.

Dionne managed to avoid major injuries during his career. As a result, he led the NHL in games played seven times. In 2017, the NHL named the Hall of Famer as one of its top 100 players of all time.

MARCEL DIONNE STATS

 Points		1,771
Goals		731
Assists		1,040
NHL All-Star Games		8

STEVE YZERMAN

Steve Yzerman played for the Detroit Red Wings from 1983 to 2006. He led Detroit to three Stanley Cup titles during that time. The Red Wings only missed the playoffs twice during Yzerman's career.

Yzerman earned the nickname The Captain because he was Detroit's team captain for 20 seasons. No other NHL player was a captain for more seasons than Yzerman was. The Hall of Famer ranks seventh all-time in points, ninth in assists, and 10th in goals.

The NHL named him one of its top 100 players of all time in 2017. Yzerman was the general manager of the Tampa Bay Lightning for eight years. He took the same position with the Red Wings in 2019.

STEVE YZERMAN STATS

Points		1,755
Goals		692
Assists		1,063
NHL All-Star Games		9

PHIL ESPOSITO

Phil Esposito began playing pro hockey in 1963. He played for the Boston Bruins, New York Rangers, and Chicago Blackhawks over 18 seasons. In 1968–1969, Esposito became the first player in NHL history to score 100 points in a season. He led the NHL in points every season from 1970–1971 through 1973–1974. Esposito is one of only four players to lead the league four years in a row. He also had a record 16 game-winning goals in two different seasons.

Esposito ranks seventh all-time in career goals and 10th in points. He also ranks fourth all-time with 118 game-winning goals. The Hall of Famer helped the Bruins win the Stanley Cup in 1970 and 1972.

Esposito became part of the Hockey Hall of Fame in 1984. His younger brother, Tony, is a Hall of Famer as well. In 2017, the NHL chose Phil Esposito as one of its top 100 players of all time.

PHIL ESPOSITO STATS

Points	1,590
Goals	717
Assists	873
NHL All-Star Games	10

SIDNEY CROSBY

The Pittsburgh Penguins chose Sidney Crosby first overall in the 2005 NHL Draft. In his first season, the 18-year-old became the youngest player to reach 100 points in a season. In 2006–2007, Crosby became the youngest player to lead the NHL in points.

Crosby was such an amazing player at a young age that he earned the nickname Sid the Kid. He has won the Hart Memorial Trophy as the NHL's MVP twice. And he led the Penguins to the Stanley Cup title three times.

At the 2010 Winter Olympic Games, Crosby scored the game-winning goal in overtime against the United States and earned a gold medal for Canada. In 2017, Sid the Kid made the NHL's top 100 players of all time list. He ranks 15th all-time in total points in the NHL.

SIDNEY CROSBY STATS

Points		1,502
Goals		550
Assists		952
NHL All-Star Games		5

Stats are accurate through the 2022–2023 NHL season.

MARK MESSIER

From 1978 to 2004, Mark Messier played 25 seasons in the NHL. Only two others played for more seasons in league history. Messier spent most of his career with the Edmonton Oilers and New York Rangers.

Messier was at his best in the playoffs. He ranks second all-time with 295 career playoff points. And he led his teams to six Stanley Cup titles. Messier is the only player in NHL history to serve as captain for two different teams that won the Stanley Cup.

Nicknamed the Moose for his strength and tough style of play, the Hall of Famer was one of the best goal scorers in league history. He ranks third all-time in points and assists and ninth in goals. In 2017, the NHL picked Messier as one of its top 100 players of all time.

MARK MESSIER STATS

Points	1,887
Goals	694
Assists	1,193
NHL All-Star Games	15

JEAN BÉLIVEAU

Jean Béliveau was one of the biggest stars of the NHL during the 1950s and 1960s. He played all 20 of his NHL seasons for the Montréal Canadiens. Béliveau was part of the Canadiens team that won five straight Stanley Cups from 1956 to 1960. For his career, he helped lead the team to 10 Stanley Cups. Only Henri Richard, Béliveau's teammate, has won more NHL titles.

The NHL listed Béliveau as one the league's top 100 players of all time in 2017. He won the Hart Trophy as the NHL's MVP twice. In 1965, he won the first Conn Smythe Trophy. This award honors the MVP of the playoffs. Béliveau helped the Canadiens win the Stanley Cup that year. He led the NHL in goals twice, assists twice, and total points once. Béliveau joined the Hockey Hall of Fame in 1972.

JEAN BÉLIVEAU STATS

Points		1,219
Goals		507
Assists		712
NHL All-Star Games		13

MARIO LEMIEUX

Mario Lemieux's size, strength, and skill made him one of the best hockey players of all time. He spent his entire 17-year career with the Pittsburgh Penguins and helped lead them to two Stanley Cup titles.

Lemieux led the NHL in points six times during his career. His 199 points in the 1988–1989 season are the fifth-most in NHL history. Lemieux battled health problems throughout his career. He missed many games, but Lemieux still ranks eighth all-time in career points.

Nicknamed Super Mario, the Hall of Famer won the Hart Trophy as the NHL's MVP three times. He's also the only player to score five kinds of goals in the same game. He scored even strength, on a power play, shorthanded, on a penalty shot, and on an empty net. Lemieux retired in 1997 and became an owner of the Penguins in 1999. In 2000, he came out of retirement and played for the team through 2005–2006. In 2017, Lemieux made the NHL's list of the 100 best players of all time.

MARIO LEMIEUX STATS

Points	1,723
Goals	690
Assists	1,033
NHL All-Star Games	10

WAYNE GRETZKY

Nicknamed the Great One, Wayne Gretzky is the greatest player ever to put on skates. He spent nine seasons with the Edmonton Oilers and led the team to four Stanley Cups. Then he played eight seasons for the Los Angeles Kings. In 1992–1993, he led the team to the Stanley Cup Finals for the first time.

The Great One is the NHL's all-time leader in points, goals, and assists. He has 936 more points than Jaromír Jágr, who is second on the list. Gretzky's assists alone would make him the league's all-time points leader.

Gretzky won nine Hart Trophies as the NHL's MVP and two Conn Smythe Trophies as MVP of the playoffs. He led the league in assists every season from 1979 to 1991.

Many believe Gretzky was the smartest player ever. He always knew where the puck was going to be. In 2017, the NHL named Gretzky the league's greatest player of all time. He joined the Hockey Hall of Fame in 1999.

WAYNE GRETZKY STATS

Points	2,857
Goals	894
Assists	1,963
NHL All-Star Games	18

EVEN MORE G.O.A.T.

There have been so many amazing centers in hockey history. Choosing only 10 is a challenge. Here are 10 others who could have made the G.O.A.T. list.

No. 11	RON FRANCIS
No. 12	STAN MIKITA
No. 13	HOWIE MORENZ
No. 14	EVGENI MALKIN
No. 15	BRYAN TROTTIER
No. 16	PETER FORSBERG
No. 17	ANGELA JAMES
No. 18	PAT LAFONTAINE
No. 19	GILBERT PERREAULT
No. 20	ERIC LINDROS

YOUR G.O.A.T.

Now it's your turn to make a G.O.A.T. list about hockey centers. Then make a list for a different hockey position! See if you can come up with other NHL G.O.A.T. lists, or even lists for other sports.

Start by doing research. You can check out the Learn More section on page 31. The books and websites listed there will help you learn more about hockey players of the past and present. You can also search online for even more information about great players.

Once you have your list, ask friends or family to create their list too. Compare them and see how they differ. Did your friends' lists make you reconsider your own? Talk it over and decide whose G.O.A.T. list is best.

GLOSSARY

assist: a pass that leads directly to a goal

draft: when teams take turns choosing new players

empty-net goal: a goal scored after one team's goalkeeper has left the goal area

even-strength goal: a goal scored when both teams have an equal number of players on the ice

general manager: someone who works for a hockey team and is in charge of decisions about players

Hall of Famer: a player who is honored in the Hockey Hall of Fame

penalty shot: a free shot at the goal allowed for certain penalties or to decide the winner of some games

point: a goal or an assist

power-play goal: a goal scored by a team that has more players on the ice

short-handed goal: a goal scored by a team that has fewer players on the ice due to a penalty

title: a championship

LEARN MORE

Britannica Kids–Ice Hockey
https://kids.britannica.com/kids/article/Ice-Hockey/353257

Doeden, Matt. *G.O.A.T. Hockey Teams*. Minneapolis: Lerner Publications, 2021.

Fishman, Jon M. *Hockey's G.O.A.T.: Wayne Gretzky, Sidney Crosby, and More*. Minneapolis: Lerner Publications, 2020.

NHL
https://www.nhl.com/

Sports Illustrated Kids–Hockey
https://www.sikids.com/hockey

Storden, Thom. *Hockey's Greatest Game-Winning Goals and Other Crunch-Time Heroics*. New York: Sports Illustrated Kids, 2020.

INDEX

PHOTO ACKNOWLEDGMENTS

Image credits: ©Mike Carlson/Stringer/Getty Images, p.4; Jason Behnken/Stringer/Getty Images, p.5; Dave Sandford/Contributor/Getty Images, p.6; Bruce Bennett/Contributor/Getty Images, p.7; Bruce Bennett/Staff/Getty Images, p.8; Andy Devlin/Contributor/Getty Images, p.9; Phillip MacCallum/Stringer/Getty Images, p.10; Richard Wolowicz/Freestyle Photo/Stringer/Getty Images, p.11; Focus On Sport/Contributor/Getty Images, p.12; Bruce Bennett/Contributor/Getty Images, p.13; Jamie Squire/Staff/Getty Images, p.14; Dave Sandford/Stringer/Getty Images, p.15; Robert Shaver/Bruce Bennett Collection/Contributor/Getty Images, p.16; Bruce Bennett/Contributor/Getty Images, p.17; Christian Petersen/Staff/Getty Images, p.18; Emilee Chinn/Stringer/Getty Images, p.19; Brian Babineau/Contributor/Getty Images, p.20; Bruce Bennett/Contributor/Getty Images, p.21; Denis Brodeur/Contributor/Getty Images, p.22; B Bennett/Contributor/Getty Images, 23; Dave Sandford/Stringer/Getty Images, p.24; Dave Sandford/Stringer/Getty Images, p.25; Steve Babineau/Contributor/Getty Images, p.26; B Bennett/Contributor/Getty Images, p.27

Cover: ©Focus Rocky W. Widner/Contributor/Getty Images; Christopher Morris - Corbis/Contributor/Getty Images; DAVID MAXWELL/Contributor/Getty Images